Martha Dandridge Custis Washington

Martha Dandridge Custis Washington

1731–1802

BY CHARNAN SIMON

CHILDREN'S PRESS®
A Division of Grolier Publishing
New York   London   Hong Kong   Sydney
Danbury, Connecticut

Consultants: ELLEN MCCALLISTER CLARK
Public Services Librarian
The Society of the Cincinnati
Washington, D.C.

LINDA CORNWELL
Coordinator of School Quality and Professional Improvement
Indiana State Teachers Association

Project Editor: DOWNING PUBLISHING SERVICES
Page Layout: CAROLE DESNOES
Photo Researcher: JAN IZZO

Visit Children's Press on the Internet at:
http://publishing.grolier.com

Library of Congress Cataloging-in-Publication Data
Simon, Charnan.
    Martha Dandridge Custis Washington, 1731–1802 / by Charnan Simon
        p. cm. — (Encyclopedia of first ladies)
    Includes bibliographical references and index.
    Summary: A biography of the wife of the first president of the United States, a woman
who did not relish her role, but who entertained her guests both warmly and formally.
    ISBN 0-516-20480-7
    1. Washington, Martha, 1731–1802—Juvenile literature. 2. Presidents' spouses—United
States—Biography—Juvenile literature. [1. Washington, Martha, 1731–1802 2. First ladies.
3. Women—Biography.] I. Title II. Series
E312.19.W34S46   2000
973.4'1'092—dc 21   99–16989
[B]   CIP
                                                 AC

GROLIER
PUBLISHING

Table of Contents

Martha Dandridge Custis Washington

CHAPTER ONE

A Pattern of Industry

The good ladies of Morristown, New Jersey, were curious—and excited. General George Washington, commander-in-chief of the Continental army, had chosen Morristown as his headquarters during this winter of 1776–1777. From the cramped rooms of Freeman Tavern, General Washington would make his plans while his army rested during their second year of fighting for American independence.

It was notable enough to have the great General Washington in Morristown. Even more exciting to the ladies, however, was the recent arrival of the general's wife. Martha Washington was one of the wealthiest women in the aristocratic state of Virginia. Whatever would such a great lady think of New Jersey society? The Morristown women took special care as they prepared to meet Lady Washington for the first time.

They were in for a surprise. As one of the ladies later explained ruefully, "I was never so ashamed in my life . . . as she was said to be so grand a lady, we thought we must put on our best bibs and bands. So we dressed ourselves in our most elegant ruffles and silks, and were introduced to her ladyship. And don't you think we found her knitting and with a specked [checked] apron on?"

Modestly dressed in brown homespun, Martha Washington greeted her visitors and then quietly resumed her knitting. Her visitors squirmed in embarrassment. "There we were without a stitch of work, and sitting in state, but General Washington's lady with her own hands was knitting stockings for herself and [her] husband."

The Morristown ladies' embarrassment just grew worse as Martha Washington gently lectured them on the proper conduct of American women. "Her ladyship took occasion to say, in a way that we could not be offended at, that at this time it was very important that American ladies should be patterns of industry to their countrymen, because the separation from the mother country will dry up the sources whence many of our comforts have been derived. We must become independent by our determination to do without what we cannot make our-

Before the war for independence, ships from Great Britain brought needed goods—and luxuries—to the colonists in America.

Panniers and Politics

✮ ✮ ✮ ✮ ✮ ✮ ✮ ✮ ✮ ✮ ✮ ✮ ✮ ✮ ✮ ✮ ✮ ✮ ✮ ✮

Before the Revolution, stylish American women looked to Europe for the latest fashions. Although colonists generally wore simpler clothing than did Europeans, wealthy people in the cities could purchase elegant foreign fabrics and accessories. Fashionable dresses reached to the ankles and were cut with very tight bodices and narrow waists. They often included a *sacque,* a kind of top layer that hung in pleats from the back and opened in the front to re-

veal a full skirt. Necklines plunged low but might be covered with a large kerchief known as a *bouffant.* Since tiny waists were very much the fashion, women laced tight girdles made of whalebone, called stays, under their dresses. At their hips, they wore pads or frames called *panniers* to extend their skirts to the sides. The wealthiest women piled their heads high with tall wigs stuffed with horsehair, topping them off with elaborate hats, veils, and other decorations. As the Revolution dawned, however, patriotic American women used fashion to make a political statement. They rejected the excesses of European dress and proudly wove and wore simple garments of homemade materials such as cotton, linen, and wool. When the British king forbade them from weaving, colonial women defied him and their homespun cloth became a symbol of the Revolution. So, while fashion-conscious ladies might have been tempted to wear fussy dresses of silk and satin, patriotic American women like Martha Washington knew better.

Conditions were brutal and food, clothing, and medicine were in short supply at the winter camp at Morristown, New Jersey, during the winter of 1776–1777.

selves. Whilst our husbands and brothers are examples of patriotism, we must be patterns of industry."

The Morristown ladies took Martha Washington's words seriously. Soon they were all knitting socks, rolling bandages from old linen tablecloths and petticoats, and organizing soup kitchens for the soldiers wintering in their community.

Conditions in Morristown were often brutal for these soldiers. Smallpox raged through the camp, and two local churches were turned into hospitals to house the sick. There were never enough supplies, no matter how often and urgently General Washington petitioned Congress for food, clothing, and medicines.

Martha Washington's heart went out to the cold, hungry, tired soldiers. Most of them were just boys, no older than her own beloved son, Jacky. Tirelessly, she visited the sick and comforted the lonely. Her plump, grandmotherly figure was soon a

American women knitted socks and made bandages from old linen tablecloths for the soldiers who were away fighting the war for independence.

much-loved sight to all the citizens of Morristown, civilian and soldier alike. As one local matron reported, "She seems very wise in experience, kind-hearted and winning in all her ways. She talked much of the suffering of the poor soldiers, especially of the sick ones. Her heart seemed to be full of compassion for them."

Nothing in Martha Dandridge Custis Washington's early life had prepared her for war. But when duty called, Martha responded with courage and compassion.

CHAPTER TWO

Young Martha

An entry in the family Bible notes that America's very first First Lady was born Martha Dandridge on June 2, 1731. The oldest of nine children, Martha —who was nicknamed Patsy—and her family lived on a plantation near the colonial capital of Williamsburg, Virginia.

The Dandridge family was not the wealthiest family in Williamsburg, but they were certainly comfortable. Martha grew up with fine furniture, elegant silk dresses, and books and toys imported from England. She took it for granted that black slaves should work in the tobacco fields and attend to household chores.

Profile of America, 1731: Americans Put Down Roots

✫ ✫

In 1731, the year Martha Dandridge was born, twelve English colonies huddled together on the eastern seaboard of the vast North American continent. Georgia wouldn't become the thirteenth colony until 1732. The lands that became Ohio were the wilderness West. Beyond them, some Spanish and French explorers penetrated the thick forests and braved the rapid rivers in search of fur, gold, and a passage to the Pacific. All the major cities—Boston, New York, Philadelphia, Williamsburg, Norfolk, Baltimore—lay near deep-sea or river ports along the East Coast. In their busy harbors, trade and travelers kept the colonies connected to Europe across the Atlantic Ocean. A handful of intrepid American settlers and explorers made their way west to the foothills of the Appalachian Mountains believing the future to lie in the "howling wilderness" beyond.

By 1731, the population of English America was doubling every 25 years, but it was not just a country of English men and women. Scotch-Irish and Germans came to escape hard times at home. Many of them came as indentured servants, signing contracts to work to pay off a debt, make good a crime, or pay back their passage to the New World. Of the total population of about 630,000, African slaves numbered 91,000. More new Americans were being born here, too, as the marriage and birth rates spiraled. Outside this new transplanted society dwelt America's original inhabitants, hundreds of diverse Native American cultures from the Abenaki to the Wampanoag. But they were already being displaced as cities grew and settlers sought land. Some tribes formed alliances with the newcomers; others moved ever farther into the forests.

Putting down roots kept Americans busy. In this handmade society, everything not imported from England was made from scratch. While most people farmed, "mechanicks" (who made things by hand), artisans, statesmen, merchants, shipbuilders, city and country folk, fishermen, and printers all found a calling here. Boston was the largest of the cities, all growing in population and sophistication.

The first public concert in America, admission five shillings, was held at a private Boston home in December 1731.

No one personified the age better than a young man named Benjamin Franklin. Curious, intelligent, and inventive, Franklin in 1731 established the first circulating library and was busy publishing *The Pennsylvania Gazette,* one of the nation's first newspapers. He later studied electricity and invented a practical stove still in use today. He became one of the nation's elder statesmen during the difficult years around the Revolution. Benjamin Franklin understood that America would succeed through ingenuity and industry.

In 1731, the war for American independence was 45 years away. For Americans in the meantime, taking root in the rugged new land was hard work enough.

Martha Dandridge was born on a plantation near the colonial capital of Williamsburg, Virginia.

As a girl, Martha was not expected to attend school. She did learn the basics of reading, writing, and arithmetic, however, probably by sitting in on lessons with her brothers' tutor. In this, she was luckier than many colonial girls, who received no formal education at all.

But Martha's most important teacher was her mother. Mrs. Dandridge taught all of her daughters to cook, sew, do fine embroidery, grow kitchen vegetables and medicinal herbs, treat household illnesses, instruct and supervise slaves—in short, to manage the households it was

The Virginia capitol at Williamsburg was built in 1705.

As part of their education, colonial women were taught to sew as well as cook and manage a household.

A woman making bread at a historic colonial house

Virginia Colony

✶ ✶

Though the colony of Virginia sprang from difficult beginnings, by the time Martha Dandridge was born there in 1731, it was the most populated and wealthy of the American colonies. Jamestown, not far from Martha's birthplace near Chesapeake Bay, had been the first permanent English settlement in America, founded in 1607. Conflict with the native Powhatan Indians, along with disease, starvation, and poor leadership, however, nearly doomed the young colony. When English merchants discovered that an Indian crop called tobacco could be sold for profit in Europe, the fortunes of the colony began to change. Up and down Virginia's Chesapeake Bay coast, tobacco planters established large farms, called plantations, where slaves and servants labored in the fields. Tobacco required so many hands to grow, harvest, and pack that by the 1700s, black people, most of them slaves, made up nearly 40 percent of Virginia's population. The largest planters kept hundreds of slaves on thousands of acres, though the Dandridge plantation, called Chestnut Grove, was of more modest size. Not far away, Williamsburg served as a center of culture, education, commerce, and government for the entire mid-Atlantic region. Indeed, Williamsburg was among the few towns in this landscape of tobacco farms and is preserved today as a fine example of colonial architecture and life.

assumed they would someday marry into.

Like other Virginia plantation young ladies, Martha also took dancing and music lessons from traveling instructors. She polished her social skills and learned the niceties of being a gracious hostess. And she was an enthusiastic and accomplished horsewoman.

Tiny, pretty, dark-haired Martha Dandridge was only seventeen years old when she attracted the notice of Daniel Parke Custis.

Custis was twenty years older than Martha—and one of the wealthiest landowners in all of Virginia. It was universally agreed that Martha Dandridge had made an excellent match

"Deputy Husbands"

✶ ✶

Colonial women worked hard. In the days before factory-made goods, American families had to raise much of their own food and make many of their own household goods. This meant that the woman, in addition to being wife and mother, made many of the things her family needed to live, from clothing to food to soap to quilts. Rural women spent much time at their spinning wheels, working wool into yarn to weave cloth; unmarried women earned the name "spinsters" for the time they spent there. Even in well-to-do families who could afford items imported from Europe, women worked hard to keep house. They maintained the household records and managed servants and slaves. Indeed, most African-American women in colonial America labored as slaves in other people's fields and kitchens.

Most Americans lived on small farms where wives and husbands toiled together. Both understood the importance of their partnership, and a wife might even be referred to as a "deputy husband." In the towns, women owned shops and taverns or worked as seamstresses. They even ran printing presses. Female midwives delivered nearly all the babies, a big job since colonial families routinely included more than eight children. In spite of their contributions to society, however, colonial women were not viewed as equals under the law. Society certainly favored men over women in matters of inheritance, authority, and education. Married women gave up all personal property and money to their husbands, and divorce was difficult to obtain. However, while men were legally more powerful, colonial American women worked just as hard to make a home in the New World. "Man may work from sun to sun, but woman's work is never done," observed a popular colonial saying.

for herself when the two were married in 1749.

Martha loved married life. She settled easily into her new husband's home and began the business of managing a plantation and slaves of her own. Best of all were the babies. As the oldest of nine children, Martha

Martha Dandridge married Daniel Parke Custis when she was eighteen.

John Parke (Jacky) Custis (left) and Martha (Patsy) Custis

was used to taking care of younger brothers and sisters. But nothing could compare with the joys of having her own children! Martha adored all her babies—Daniel, born in 1751, Frances, born in 1753, John (called Jacky), born in 1754, and Martha (called Patsy), born in 1756.

So Martha was heartbroken when Daniel died when he was just two years old. Her sorrow intensified when little Frances died shortly before her fourth birthday. And she was devastated when, barely three months after the death of Frances, her husband died in July of 1757. Martha was just twenty-six years old, and her life had come crashing down around her.

✯ ✯ ✯ ✯ ✯ ✯ ✯ ✯ ✯ ✯ ✯ ✯ ✯ ✯

CHAPTER THREE

George and Martha

✫ ✫ ✫ ✫ ✫ ✫ ✫ ✫ ✫ ✫ ✫ ✫ ✫ ✫ ✫

Martha Custis had little time to mourn. Daniel had left her with an enormous estate to manage. His plantation was really many farms, spread over 17,000 acres (6,880 hectares) across six Virginia counties. Daniel's trusted business manager stayed on to advise Martha, but the final decisions regarding the household, the vast tobacco fields, and the hundreds of black slaves, were Martha's.

Valiantly, Martha coped as best she could. She was determined to carry on the family tobacco business. The few surviving letters from that period of her life show her busily writing to Daniel's business agents in

✫ ✫ ✫ ✫ ✫ ✫ ✫ ✫ ✫ ✫ ✫ ✫ ✫ ✫ ✫

According to family lore, Colonel George Washington's first meeting with Martha Dandridge Custis took place at the home of a mutual friend.

Martha Dandridge Custis, widow of Daniel Parke Custis, had two children when she married George Washington on January 6, 1759.

London: "I shall yearly ship a considerable part of the Tobacco . . . which I shall take care to have made as good as possible and hope you will do your endeavor to get me a good Price."

But Martha was not to remain a widow for long. No one knows exactly when she met the man who would become her second husband and the first president of the United States. Family lore has it that Martha Custis was staying at the home of a friend when George Washington, a colonel in the Virginia militia and hero of the

George Washington at the age of twenty-five

Washington's Other War

✶ ✶

By the 1750s, the world realized that the North American continent was a land of abundant natural resources, including furs and timber. Even though British colonies occupied the eastern seaboard, the French explored and claimed the lands to the west and into Canada. They made allies of the Native Americans, and they built forts and fur-trading outposts throughout the wilderness. This angered the British, who also wanted to control those rich lands. Finally, in 1753, the British sent troops from the Virginia colony under the leadership of a twenty-two-year-old officer named George Washington to confront the French at Fort Duquesne (near present-day Pittsburgh). The encounter led to the first and only surrender of Washington's career. (The French graciously released Washington and his men with full honors.) The following year, Washington rode against the fort again with General Edward Braddock and 2,400 men. French soldiers and Indian warriors experienced in wilderness fighting defeated them in a surprise attack and killed Braddock. Washington led the remaining troops in an orderly retreat. He later wrote his mother, "The Virginia troops showed a good deal of bravery, and were near all killed. . . . I luckily escaped without a wound, though I had four bullets through my coat, and two horses shot under me." Washington served as commander of the Virginia forces until 1758 when he resigned, unhappy with the British treatment of their colonial soldiers. By 1763, the British had succeeded in driving the French from North America.

French and Indian War, stopped by for dinner. There was an immediate attraction between the two young people and within a few short weeks, Martha had accepted George's proposal of marriage.

Martha Dandridge Custis married George Washington on January 6, 1759. The bride wore elegant yellow brocade, but even in lavender silk high-heeled slippers, she barely came up to her new husband's shoulder. (Al-

George Washington and the Custis children, Jacky and Patsy, are shown here with Mount Vernon field hands during a tour of the plantation.

though many future portrait painters would show the couple as being similar in height, Martha stood barely 5 feet (152 centimeters) tall, while George was 6 feet 2 inches (188 cm).

By now, George had resigned his commission in the Virginia militia and had been elected to the state legislature. The young couple spent the first few months of their marriage in the Custis mansion in Williamsburg, where George was sworn into the Virginia House of Burgesses.

In April 1759, George took his bride and her two children—five-year-old Jacky and three-year-old Patsy—to Mount Vernon, his family plantation in northern Virginia. For the next forty years, Martha Washington would call this lovely, gracious house overlooking the Potomac River home.

Martha and George soon settled into a pleasant routine. Almost immediately, a long list of household goods was ordered from George's agent in London. It would take nearly a year

The House of Burgesses

✮ ✮

In the summer of 1619, the first representative legislature in the New World met in a Jamestown, Virginia, church. In a way, that meeting set in motion the events that would lead to the American Revolution more than 150 years later. The Virginia House of Burgesses, as this general assembly came to be called, along with a royal governor appointed by the English king and a council of advisers governed the colony of Virginia. At annual meetings, "burgesses" (an English word for representatives) elected from the community worked to represent the people of Virginia in matters of taxation and lawmaking. Because the right to vote was limited to landowning white males, the House of Burgesses' early members were mostly wealthy plantation owners. They were nonetheless a stubborn lot who demanded control of their local government. Over the years, this created many problems with the British king, who was reluctant to give up authority over the colonies. Trouble brewing in the House of Burgesses and in other colonial assemblies reached a fever pitch in 1765 when statesman Patrick Henry delivered a rousing speech against taxation of printed documents, called the Stamp Act, by the English Crown. And it was the feisty Virginia burgesses who called for a meeting of representatives from all the colonies in 1774 at the first Continental Congress to protest British rule.

for this order to make its way across the Atlantic Ocean and up the Potomac River to Mount Vernon's private landing dock. When it finally arrived, it contained everything from perfumed powder to plows, from satin ribbons to salt, from children's books to Cheshire cheeses.

While George managed the plantation's several farms, Martha ran the Mount Vernon household. She set some slaves to spinning, weaving, and sewing, and others to washing and cleaning. She supervised the kitchen slaves and made sure the kitchen herb and vegetable gardens were well-tended. She kept an especially close eye on the smokehouse, where the

A 1792 painting attributed to Edward Savage of Mount Vernon depicts George Washington's lovely, gracious home overlooking the Potomac River.

A huge order of household goods ordered from Washington's agent in London directly after George and Martha were married was delivered nearly a year later to Mount Vernon's private landing dock.

Handmade, Homemade

✳ ✳

Colonial Americans lived in a handmade and homemade society. Women learned, or devised, "receipts" (recipes) for everything from candles to wrinkle cream. One book called *The Toilet of Flora* contained a collection of "receipts for cosmetics of every Kind, that can smooth and brighten the Skin, give Force to BEAUTY, and take off the Appearance of OLD AGE and DECAY." Without benefit of store-bought air fresheners or toothpastes, Martha Washington blended these favorite concoctions:

"A Perfume to Stand in a Room: Take three quarts of rose buds & put them in a pot with bay salt, 4 grayns of musk & ambergreece, 30 drops of oyle of rodium, a little benjamin & storeax, & keep it allways close covered, but when you have a mind to have yr roome sweet you must take of ye cover.

To Keep Teeth Clean & White and to Fasten Them: Take cuttle fishbone and make it into a very fine powder & rub ye teeth well with a cloth, then wash them after with white wine & it will preserf ye teeth & keep them white & clean & preserf from ye toothach iff it be used every day."

Unfortunately, the toothpaste seems to have been less than successful since both Martha and George wore false teeth.

fine Virginia hams and bacons were aged. As George would write to a friend, "Virginia ladies value themselves on the goodness of their bacon."

In all that she did, Martha proved herself an able manager—energetic, self-disciplined, and competent. If she had any weakness, it showed itself where her children were concerned.

For try as she might, Martha couldn't help spoiling Jacky and Patsy. Perhaps it was because Martha still felt the loss of her first two children so keenly. Perhaps it was her own generous nature or her understandable desire to spare her children the sorrow she had known. Whatever the reason, Martha was an extraordinarily indulgent mother.

Martha Washington
supervised the slaves
who worked in the
Mount Vernon
kitchen, now restored
(above).

She also made sure
that the kitchen herb
and vegetable gardens
(left) were well-
tended.

This was especially noticeable with Jacky. Martha lavished her son with gifts and could never make the easygoing Jacky do anything he didn't want to do. First with his tutor, and later when he went away to school, Jacky proved to be an indifferent scholar. He much preferred fox hunting to studying mathematics and Latin. Charming and affectionate to his mother, Jacky spent much of his youth promising to try harder—and then failing to live up to his promises.

Of greater concern was Patsy. Always frail in health, Patsy began suffering from epileptic seizures when she was twelve years old. Martha consulted the best doctors in Virginia and tried every cure that was suggested, but nothing helped. Patsy's health was a continual source of worry and anxiety to her loving mother.

Life at Mount Vernon was not all work and worry, however. The Washingtons entertained frequently, and their plantation home was often bursting with houseguests who stayed for weeks at a time. Plantation records show that between 1768 and 1775, the Washingtons entertained more

John (Jacky) Custis

Martha (Patsy) Custis

Epilepsy

★ ★

Over the years, the brain disorder known today as epilepsy has been greatly feared and misunderstood. Because epilepsy's disturbing symptoms can include uncontrollable convulsions, or seizures, people sometimes believed epileptics to be insane. The ancient Greeks called epilepsy "the sacred disease" because they thought epileptics had been touched by the gods. Medieval Europeans believed just the opposite, fearing that people undergoing epileptic fits were possessed by demons. In early America, epileptics were sometimes suspected of witchcraft. Doctors in Martha's day could do little to relieve or cure the affliction, and families no doubt felt helpless and frightened when loved ones suffered from epileptic seizures. More than 200 years later, a tool called an electroencephalograph was invented that shed some light on the mysterious illness. The device recorded electrical activity in the brain and showed that epileptic seizures are caused by disturbed electrical rhythms there. Epilepsy remains a serious affliction, but many of the 2.3 million Americans who suffer from it today are able to control their symptoms with drugs, surgery, and careful diets.

than 2,000 visitors! Neighborhood fox hunts, boat races, and dances were popular, and nearby Alexandria and Williamsburg offered a variety of theatrical amusements. And though Martha lived too far away from her family to see them more than once a year or so, she kept up a lively correspondance with favored friends and relatives. All in all, Martha's early married years with George Washington were busy and happy.

By the mid-1760s, however, public events were beginning to intrude on Martha Washington's private happiness. Relations between England and the colonies were strained, and George Washington was in the thick of the political unrest.

In 1765, the British Parliament

Between 1768 and 1775, the Washingtons entertained more than 2,000 visitors at Mount Vernon, many of whom stayed for weeks at a time.

passed the Stamp Act, which taxed newspapers, legal documents, and other printed material. To protest, colonists organized a boycott of British-made goods, and the Stamp Act was repealed in 1766.

The relief was short-lived. In 1767, Parliament passed the Townshend Acts, which taxed lead, paint, paper, and tea imported into the colonies. There were more protests, and the British sent troops into Boston and

Stamp Act protesters throughout the colonies organized a boycott of British-made goods and rioted in Boston (above).

Paul Revere's engraving of the Boston Massacre, in which British troops killed five civilians who were protesting the Townshend Acts

On December 16, 1773, a group of Boston rebels (many of whom dressed themselves as American Indians) dumped a shipload of tea into Boston Harbor in protest of the British tax on tea.

New York City. When British troops in Boston killed five civilians on March 5, 1770, in what became known as the Boston Massacre, British and American citizens alike were outraged.

Partly in response to the Boston Massacre, Parliament repealed the Townshend Acts—all except the tax on imported tea. When a group of Boston rebels protested by dumping a shipload of tea into Boston Harbor

on December 16, 1773, Parliament promptly closed Boston Harbor and passed a series of restrictive acts known to the colonists as the Intolerable Acts.

Both George and Martha had close ties to England. They had friends and family who lived or had studied in the mother country. They depended on Britain for the luxury items they both so enjoyed. But the Washingtons were

Americans first and foremost. They approved the boycott of British-made goods. They shared their fellow colonists' indignation about taxation without representation. As a soldier, George had even begun to think about waging war against Britain, if that's what it would take to secure the colonists' rights.

Martha had more urgent personal matters on her mind. First, eighteen-year-old Jacky wanted to quit school and marry a charming fifteen-year-old named Nelly Calvert. George was strongly opposed to the marriage and to the idea of Jacky quitting college. But Martha, who had been only eighteen when she married the first time, could never deny her darling Jacky anything. She only reluctantly agreed that the marriage should be postponed until Jacky had finished college in New York.

Patsy was also causing Martha increasing concern. Her seizures were coming more and more frequently. Martha despaired of her daughter ever growing up to live a normal life.

Martha's worst fears were realized on a warm June evening in 1773.

Mount Vernon was filled with visitors—George's brother's family, Jacky's fiancée Nelly, and many friends. After a lively family dinner, seventeen-year-old Patsy rose from the table—and suffered her most severe seizure yet. Within minutes, Patsy was dead. Martha was devastated.

As George wrote to his brother-in-law: "She rose from Dinner about four o'clock in better health and spirits than she appeared to have been in for

George's brother Lawrence was among the guests at Mount Vernon on the evening Patsy died.

✮ ✮

"My Dearest: I am now set down to write you on a subject which fills me with inexpressible concern—and this concern is greatly aggravated and Increased when I reflect upon the uneasiness I know it will give you—It has been determined in Congress, that the whole Army raised for the defence of the American Cause shall be put under my care, and that it is necessary for me to proceed immediately to Boston to take upon me the Command of it. You may believe me my dear Patcy . . . I have used every endeavour in my power to avoid it, not only from my unwillingness to part with you and the Family, but from a consciousness of its being a trust too great for my Capacity and that I should enjoy more real happiness and felicity in one month with you, at home, than I have the most distant prospect of reaping abroad, if my stay were to be Seven times Seven years. But, as it has been a kind of destiny that has thrown me upon this Service, I shall hope that my undertaking of it, is designed to answer some good purpose . . . and it was utterly out of my power to

some time; soon after which she was seiced with one of her usual Fits, and expired in it, in less than two minutes without uttering a word, a groan, or scarce a sigh. This sudden, and unexpected blow, I scarce need add has almost reduced my poor Wife to the lowest ebb of Misery; which is encreas'd by the absence of her son, (whom I have just fixed at the College in New York . . .) and want of the balmy consolation of her Relations,

which leads me more than ever to wish she could see them."

After Patsy's death, Martha missed Jacky more than ever. She saw no reason he should stay in a college he disliked in New York, when he could be married to his sweetheart and settled near his mother in Virginia. By December, George Washington accepted defeat in the matter of Jacky's marriage. As he wrote to the president of Jacky's college, "I have yielded con-

refuse this appointment without exposing my Character to such censures as would have reflected dishonour upon myself, and given pain to my friends . . . . I shall rely therefore, confidently, on that Providence which has heretofore preservd, & been bountiful to me, not doubting but that I shall return safe to you in the fall. . . . My unhappiness will flow from the uneasiness I know you will feel at being left alone— I therefore beg of you to summon your whole fortitude & Resolution, and pass your time as agreeably as possible. . . .

As Life is always uncertain, and common prudence dictates to every Man the necessity of settling his temporal Concerns whilst it is in his power—and while the Mind is calm and undisturbed, I have, since I came to this place . . . got Col. Pendleton to Draft a Will for me by the directions which I gave him which will I now Inclose—The Provision made for you, in cas(e) of my death will, I hope be agreeable. . . . I shall . . . assure you that I am with the most unfeigned regard, My dear Patcy Yr Affecte Go: Washington.

P.S. Since writing the above I have receivd your Letter of the 15th and have got two suits of . . . the prettiest Muslin. I wish it may please you . . ."

trary to my judgment, and much against my wishes to his quitting College; in order that he may enter soon into a new scene of Life, which I think he would be much fitter for some years hence, than now, but having his own inclination, the desires of his mother and the acquiessence of almost all his relatives, to encounter, I did not care, as he is the last of the family, to push my opposition too far; and therefore have submitted to a Kind of necessity."

George may have had other things on his mind besides Jacky's marriage. Certainly he had good reasons to want to make Martha happy at this particular time. He better than anyone foresaw how drastically life at Mount Vernon would change in the near future.

In September 1774, George Washington was a delegate to the first Continental Congress when it met in Philadelphia to discuss what to do about problems with Britain. By early

The Philadelphia State House (later called Independence Hall) was the site of the Second Continental Congress, which named George Washington commander-in-chief of the Continental army.

1775, Washington was in Virginia recruiting and training troops in preparation for war. When the Second Continental Congress met in the spring of 1775, George Washington was named commander-in-chief of the newly formed Continental army.

Washington left Philadelphia almost immediately to take command of the army in Massachusetts. It would be six long years before he returned to Mount Vernon even for a visit. It would be eight years before he returned home to live.

In the meantime, Martha Washington would carry on alone. Once again, her life had been turned upside-down by events beyond her control.

George Washington, the new commander-in-chief, takes charge of the Continental army.

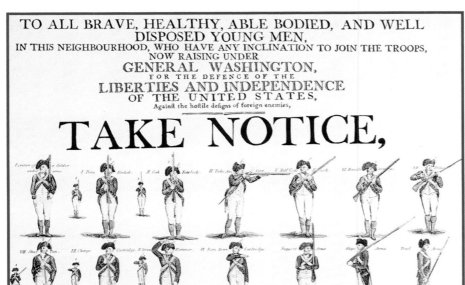

TO ALL BRAVE, HEALTHY, ABLE BODIED, AND WELL DISPOSED YOUNG MEN,
IN THIS NEIGHBOURHOOD, WHO HAVE ANY INCLINATION TO JOIN THE TROOPS,
NOW RAISING UNDER
GENERAL WASHINGTON,
FOR THE DEFENCE OF THE
LIBERTIES AND INDEPENDENCE
OF THE UNITED STATES,
Against the hostile designs of foreign enemies,

TAKE NOTICE,

An American Revolution recruiting poster urging young men to join General George Washington in the war for independence

41

CHAPTER FOUR

War!

George Washington was clearly worried about Martha being left alone at Mount Vernon while he went to war. There were rumors that Martha might be taken hostage by hostile British forces, or that Mount Vernon itself might come under attack. Concerned for his wife's happiness and well-being, Washington urged Martha to stay with family members until he could return.

While Martha was happy to pay a short visit to her favorite sister Nancy, she had no intention of abandoning the home that she and George loved so dearly. She was delighted when Jacky and Nelly moved back

General George Washington stopping at an inn on the way to his winter headquarters in Cambridge

Martha traveled in this carriage to be with George at his headquarters in Cambridge, Massachusetts.

to Mount Vernon to keep her company. She determined to do her best to keep the plantation running smoothly in her husband's absence.

There was only one thing that could convince Martha to leave home for any length of time. So when George wrote in October 1775 asking her to join him at his winter headquarters in Cambridge, Massachusetts, Martha went to her husband's side.

It was no small feat, traveling the 500 miles (805 kilometers) or so from Virginia to Massachusetts in winter, particularly for a woman who had never been north of Alexandria in her life. But Martha never uttered a word of complaint, and was indeed touched by the reception she received all along the route. Colonists everywhere were honored to meet General Washing-

The American Revolution: Fast Facts

WHAT: The war for American independence

WHEN: 1775–1783

WHO: Between Britain and the thirteen American colonies. France and Spain joined the war in support of the colonies in 1778.

WHERE: Along the East Coast of North America, and as far west as Indiana, with major battles in Massachusetts, New York, New Jersey, Pennsylvania, the Carolinas, Virginia, and Canada.

WHY: Began as a dispute between colonists and king over Britain's authority and its power to tax and control trade in the American colonies. On July 4, 1776, when leading American patriots signed the Declaration of Independence, everything changed. Now, the colonists were fighting for their independence from Britain.

OUTCOME: An American victory at Yorktown, Virginia, ended the fighting, but it took two more years for a treaty to be signed. Finally, in 1783, England recognized the United States of America with the Treaty of Paris.

General George Washington and others at the Cambridge, Massachusetts, Continental army camp during the winter of 1775–1776

ton's wife, and Martha said she was treated "as if I had been a very great somebody."

Cambridge was a different story. Martha was always happiest at her husband's side, and she did her best to create a homelike atmosphere in the grim army headquarters. But she couldn't entirely hide her shock and sorrow at the sights and sounds of war. As she wrote to a friend shortly after her arrival in Cambridge, "I have waited some days to collect something to tell, but alas there is nothing but what you will find in the papers . . . some days we have a number of cannon and shells from Boston and Bunkers Hill, but it does not seem to surprise any one but me; I confess I shudder every time I hear the sound of a gun . . . to me that never see any thing of war, the preparations, are very terable indeed, but I endever to keep my fears to myself as well as I can."

With this visit to Cambridge, Martha Washington established a pattern that would continue for eight long years of fighting. Every winter,

Becoming Americans

☆ ☆

When Great Britain ruled the American colonies, the people who lived here were British citizens. By 1774, colonists had grown angry over high taxes and British control over their lives. They felt unfairly treated. To discuss these problems, more than forty delegates from around the colonies met at Philadelphia's Carpenters' Hall in the first Continental Congress. They made some demands, but Britain ignored them. The Second Continental Congress met in 1775, and took stronger action by electing George Washington as commander of forces "to be raised for the defence of American liberty." Finally, the Congress stopped insisting that the colonists be treated fairly as British citizens. On July 4, 1776, they signed the Declaration of Independence, demanding the freedom and independence of the "thirteen united States of America." No longer British citizens, the colonists from then on would be Americans.

During the miserable winter of 1777–1778, Martha Washington tended to sick and wounded soldiers at the Valley Forge Continental army camp.

she traveled from Mount Vernon to wherever George had established his winter headquarters. Every spring, when the fighting started up again, Martha would make the long, hard journey back home. Cambridge, Morristown, Valley Forge, Middlebrook, New Windsor, Philadelphia, Newburgh, Princeton—the cold northern cities must have seemed strange indeed to this gentle southern woman.

Gentle and sheltered though she may have been, Martha Washington did her wartime duty cheerfully and energetically. The Morristown ladies weren't the only ones impressed by the general's hardworking wife. As a woman in Valley Forge wrote of the miserable winter of 1777–1778, "I never in my life knew a woman so busy from early morning until late at night as was Lady Washington, pro-

The Winters of War

✯ ✯

Washington's Continental army endured eight winters of revolution. In the cold weather and deep snows, marching and fighting became nearly impossible and fresh food for men and horses dwindled. So, at winter's freeze, the armies hunkered down in winter encampments, sometimes called cantonments, to await the

spring thaw. Perhaps the best known of Washington's winter camps is Valley Forge, Pennsylvania, where he and 12,000 exhausted men dug in to wait. Washington begged Congress for provisions for his starving and ill-clad troops. "You might have tracked the army to Valley Forge by the blood of their feet," he said. Two years later, troops at Morristown, New Jersey, weathered twenty-six snowstorms in crude log huts. Washington stayed in a local home, planning the spring campaign and worrying about his troops. Miraculously, only 86 of nearly 13,000 perished that year. During the final

winter of the war, the army camped at New Windsor, New York, where they restlessly awaited the signing of the peace treaty. Though the troops were well housed and clothed that winter, only Washington's skillful appeals kept his homesick men from mutiny over back pay. Indeed, while the Revolution might easily have been lost during those difficult winters, George Washington's leadership held his army together. And, by all accounts, Martha's warm presence in those dismal camps lifted the spirits of soldiers and officers alike.

General Washington visiting wounded soldiers at Valley Forge

Washington's headquarters at Valley Forge

viding comforts for the sick soldiers. . . . Every fair day she might be seen, with basket in hand, and with a single attendant, going among the huts seeking the keenest and most needy suf-

ferer, and giving all the comforts to him in her power."

Besides tending to the sick and wounded common soldiers' needs, Martha did her best to brighten up the officers' quarters. She never arrived at winter camp empty-handed, and the good Mount Vernon hams and bacons, cheeses, nuts, and dried fruits did much to improve army food. With other officers' wives, Martha organized dinner parties, horseback rides, and even—knowing how much George loved the minuet—an occasional dance.

Mainly, though, Martha offered

During her time at winter camps, Martha organized many activities, including an occasional dance.

comfort and support to her husband. The Continental army was a ragtag one, poorly trained and even more poorly financed by Congress. There was never enough food, never enough ammunition, never enough shoes or blankets or horses. Leading such an army to victory was a daunting task, and George Washington's letters show him to be a frequently frustrated general. Throughout the Revolutionary War, Martha Washington worked tire-lessly to provide an oasis of peace and comfort for her husband.

When Martha was not working hard at winter camp, she was working hard at home. She had successfully undergone the still-experimental smallpox inoculation in May of 1776. The following summer, she held an informal family smallpox clinic at Mount Vernon. It was a wonderful opportunity for the motherly Martha to invite several nieces and nephews to spend the summer with her. She missed the children when they went home.

As she wrote her sister Nancy following the visit by Nancy's two sons, "My Dear Sister, I have the very great pleasure of returning you your Boys as well as they were when I brought them from Eltham—They have had the small pox exeeding light and have been perfectly well this fortnight past . . . they have been exeeding good Boys indeed and I shall hope you will lett them come to see me when ever they can spare so much time from school—they have been such good Boys that I shall love them a great deal more than I ever did . . ."

51

Smallpox

✶ ✶

Smallpox was among the most feared diseases of the eighteenth century. It could spread through the air very quickly from a single infected person and cause city-wide epidemics like the one that killed 800 people in Boston in 1721. Introduced into the New World by Europeans, the disease wiped out entire groups of Native Americans. Those the disease didn't kill, it scarred with pockmarks for life. People knew little about the virus and doctors had no cure, but they did realize that those who lived through it never got it again. In fact, servants with pockmarks often made higher wages because employers knew they would not contract the dis-

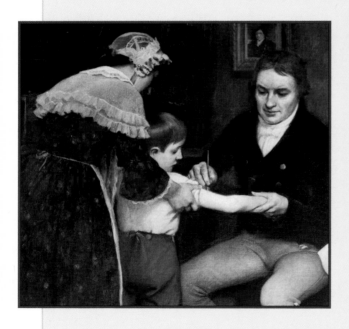

ease. Even among aristocrats, a mildly pocked face was not undesirable; George Washington himself bore the scars of the disease. In the early 1700s, some people came to believe that introducing a small amount of pus from a smallpox sore under a healthy person's skin would create a mild case of infection and make that person immune to the disease. The procedure, called inoculation, was controversial, however, because there was no way to control an individual's reaction. Nonetheless, while it caused some deaths, the crude preventive often worked. In 1796, Englishman Edward Jenner discovered a more effective treatment that involved inoculating people with a milder version of the disease common in cows. The procedure came to be called *vaccination*, derived from the Latin word for cow, and it virtually eliminated the frightening killer disease.

There were other projects and pleasures, too. Before the war, George Washington had begun building several additions to Mount Vernon. During his absence, Martha made sure the remodeling continued.

Even more exciting was Jacky and Nelly's growing family. Baby Eliza (called Betsy or Beth) was born in the summer of 1776; Martha (nicknamed Patty) followed in 1777; Eleanor (Nelly) arrived in 1779; and George Washington Parke (nicknamed Wash) was born in 1781. Although Jacky and his brood did not live with Martha, they visited frequently. Baby Nelly, in fact, spent much of her infancy at Mount Vernon, after her mother proved too weak and ill to nurse her.

When Martha was not at home with her loved ones, she thought of them constantly and wrote frequently. She longed for news of Jack, Nelly, and the children and grew anxious if that news was not forthcoming. She was not above a gentle scolding if the situation warranted! As she wrote in March 1779 from Middlebrook, New Jersey: "My Dear Children, Not having received any letter from you, the

AUGUSTINE WASHINGTON'S HOUSE
c.1735 TO 1757

MIDDLE PERIOD
1758 TO 1774

FINAL DEVELOPMENT
1774 TO 1799

These sketches show the various stages of Mount Vernon's transformation between 1735 and 1799.

53

To Martha's delight, her son Jacky, his wife Nelly, and their children spent many lengthy visits with George and Martha at Mount Vernon.

two last posts—I have only to tell you, that the general & my self are well . . . I hear so very seldom from you, that I don't know where you are or weather you intend to come to Alexandria to live this spring or when. . . . The last letter from Nelly she now says Boath the children have been very ill, they were she hoped getting better—if you doe not write to me—I will not write to you again . . . give the dear little girls a kiss for me, and tell Beth I have got a pritty new doll for her . . ."

Martha was home at Mount Vernon when unexpected good news arrived in September of 1781. George was coming home! Not alone and not for long, but after six long years,

Eliza (Betsy) Parke Custis

George Washington (Wash) Parke Custis

Eleanor (Nelly) Parke Custis

George Washington would finally be eating at his own table and sleeping in his own bed. He and his officers would stop at Mount Vernon for three days on their way to an important battle in Yorktown, Virginia. Hurriedly, preparations were made, and Jacky, Nelly, and four excited children were summoned to meet their grandfather for the first time.

By that fall of 1781, the tide was

On October 19, 1781, after what was to be the last battle of the American Revolutionary War, British general Cornwallis surrendered to American general George Washington at Yorktown, Virginia.

beginning to turn in the Revolutionary War. The French had joined the war on the American side, and George Washington was hopeful that the combined American and French forces would soon defeat the British.

When Martha waved good-bye to her husband after his too-short visit, she also sent her only son off to war. Jacky Custis had spent the early years of the war managing his affairs, raising his family, and attending to his mother. Now, he wanted to see some battle action. His proud stepfather

made him an aide, and the two set off to Yorktown together.

George Washington's victory at the Battle of Yorktown was decisive and triumphant. Thousands of British troops under General Cornwallis's command surrendered their arms on October 19, 1781. Though the two armies did not yet know it, this would be the last major battle of the American Revolutionary War.

The triumph of Yorktown soon turned tragic for Martha and George Washington. Twenty-eight-year-old

General George Washington dancing at a victory ball after the surrender of Cornwallis

George and Martha at the deathbed of Jacky Custis, who died of camp fever in Yorktown seventeen days after the surrender of Cornwallis

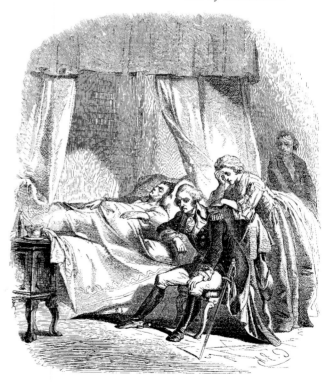

Jacky Custis had been with his stepfather's army for only a few short weeks when he caught camp fever. George Washington recognized the seriousness of the young man's illness and sent for Martha, Nelly, and five-year-old Eliza. But even the most devoted nursing could not save the young man. On November 5, 1781, Jacky Custis died, surrounded by those who loved him best. Martha Washington had outlived all of her children.

The next two years were long and dreary ones for Martha Washington. For all practical purposes, the Revolutionary War ended at Yorktown. But it wasn't until the Treaty of Paris was signed in 1783 that peace was

The Treaty of Paris

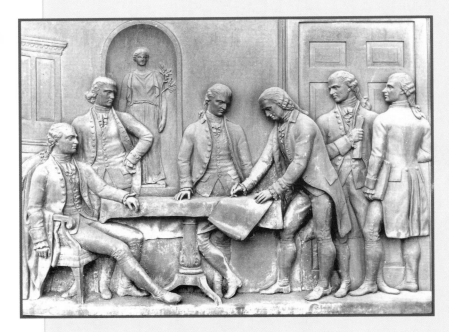

Though nobody knew it was over, the Revolution petered out after the American victory at Yorktown in October 1781. When the British admitted defeat several months later, the complicated peace process could begin. Congress sent a fine team of negotiators to Paris—Benjamin Franklin, John Jay, and John Adams—to hammer out a treaty granting the American colonies their independence. It was a tricky businesss. Rumors flew that European nations would conspire to deny the claim; after all, the North American continent offered much that Europeans wanted. France, America's ally, delayed the talks for months until other matters had been settled among themselves, Britain, and Spain. Other European nations jostled to protect their interests. Conflicts arose over how far west America should extend, and French negotiators suggested that the British should keep New York City. Frustrated, the Americans opened secret talks directly with the British. England agreed to complete independence and to set the western boundary of the United States at the Mississippi River. Americans rejoiced over the splendid terms, and when the French finally reached their own agreement with Britain, the treaty was signed on September 3, 1783.

At Annapolis, Maryland, on December 23, 1783, General George Washington resigned his commission as commander-in-chief of the Continental army.

officially declared. Until that time, Martha continued joining her husband in his army camp for part of the year, and spending the rest of the year at Mount Vernon.

Finally, in December of 1783, Martha's long wartime service ended. In a moving ceremony in the capitol in Annapolis, Maryland, on December 23, George Washington resigned his commission in the Continental army with these words: "Having now finished the work assigned me, I retire from the great theatre of action."

Martha was not there to hear George speak. As always, her first concern was the domestic comfort and happiness of those she loved. While George addressed his public, Martha was at Mount Vernon preparing for his homecoming. By the time George arrived on Christmas Eve 1783, Martha had the house ready and Nelly and the four grandchildren eagerly waiting to greet their grandfather. Perhaps now, at last, Martha Washington could enjoy some hard-earned peace and quiet.

CHAPTER FIVE

"My Little Family Are All With Me"

★ ★ ★ ★ ★ ★ ★ ★ ★ ★ ★ ★ ★ ★ ★ ★ ★ ★

Martha and George Washington quickly settled into a happy domestic routine which must have seemed luxurious compared to the hardships of war. After years of personal sacrifice and public service, they both wanted nothing more than to spend the rest of their lives at Mount Vernon—or, as Martha put it in a letter, "to grow old in solitude and tranquility together."

Mount Vernon had deteriorated during their absence. The fields and buildings all suffered from neglect, but George was determined to bring the plantation back to peak condition. This was as much a financial neccessity

★ ★ ★ ★ ★ ★ ★ ★ ★ ★ ★ ★ ★ ★ ★ ★ ★ ★

George Washington Slept Here

✷ ✷

George Washington spent much of his childhood at Mount Vernon, his half-brother's home on the banks of the Potomac River, and he inherited the property in 1761. He loved the estate with a passion, and though he devoted much of his life to serving his country, his first love was farming, the "most delectable" occupation. Throughout his life, he enlarged and improved Mount Vernon, increasing its lands to 8,000 acres (3,238 ha) divided into several farms worked by some 200 slaves. Washington himself experimented with crop rotation and new varieties of plants. Everywhere, the grounds of Mount Vernon hummed with activity. Cobblers, weavers, ironmongers, and blacksmiths made it a self-sufficient community, as was typical of southern plantations of the day. From her desk in the second-floor master bedchamber, Martha ran the household and supervised the 90 slaves who worked in the mansion. She liked to describe herself as "an old-fashioned Virginia housekeeper, steady as a clock, busy as a bee, and cheerful as a cricket." George and Martha welcomed guests at Mount Vernon and would be pleased to know that since 1858 the estate has been open for all Americans to enjoy. Today, it is the country's most visited historic home, and its familiar red roof, cupola, and simple classical style have made it the most familiar house in America.

as a matter of pride. By his own request, George Washington had not received any salary during his years as commander-in-chief of the Continental army. He had donated much of his personal fortune, as well as his time and energies, to the revolutionary cause. Now the time had come to repair his losses.

Martha, too, was happily occupied from morning until night with her gardens, her spinning wheels, her smokehouse, and her needlework. It was with great satisfaction and joy that Martha resumed her beloved homey duties.

Best of all, there were once again

George and Martha with their grandchildren Nelly and Wash, who lived at Mount Vernon after the death of their father Jacky

children to care for at Mount Vernon. Jacky's youngest children, little Nelly and Wash (sometimes affectionately known as "Tub"), had spent much of their infancy at Mount Vernon when their mother was too weak and ill to nurse them. Now, the senior Nelly was well and had remarried. The two old- est daughters, Eliza and Patty, lived with their mother and stepfather. But Martha and George were allowed to keep the two youngest children to raise at Mount Vernon. There was much visiting back and forth between the two families, and everyone was happy with the arrangement.

George and Martha Washington celebrated their twenty-fifth wedding anniversary in 1784 with a reception for family and friends at Mount Vernon.

Martha loved having Nelly and Wash to care for. She watched over them endlessly, and nothing gave her greater pleasure than to be able to write to a friend, "My little family are all with me, and have been very well . . ."

But Martha worried as well as watched. Good health was never to be taken for granted in eighteenth-century America, as Martha knew to her sorrow. She herself had already lost all four of her own children to illness, plus five of her brothers and

sisters and numerous nieces and nephews. So it was with real concern that she wrote to her favorite niece, Fanny, "My Dear little children have all been very well, till today my pritty little Dear Boy complains of a pain in his stomach. I hope it proceeds from cold as he is much better than he was some months agoe and a good nights sleep I trust will carry of his complaints altogether—I cannot say but it makes me miserable if ever he complains let the cause be ever so trifel-

George Washington, now retired from the army, and his wife Martha enjoying breakfast with their grand-children Nelly and Wash at Mount Vernon in 1786

ing—I hope the almighty will spare him to me . . ."

Besides the babies, Martha loved to surround herself with companionable young people. There were usually several nieces and nephews visiting or living at Mount Vernon. Martha's favorite was always Fanny Bassett, daughter of Martha's beloved sister Nancy, who had died in 1778. With Fanny's help, Martha continued the tradition of hospitality she had always practiced at Mount Vernon. Meals were bountiful, and guests frequently slept four to a room.

As George Washington himself humorously described Mount Vernon during this period, it was like "a well-

resorted tavern, as scarcely any travelers who are going from north to south or south to north do not spend a day or two in it." And when the day came in June of 1785 that there were no visitors, George found the occasion notable enough to enter in his diary: "Dined with only Mrs. Washington, which I believe is the first instance of it since my retirement from public life."

Unfortunately for Martha, many of her houseguests came to talk politics with George. The American people

Martha Washington's favorite niece, Fanny Bassett, was the daughter of her beloved sister Nancy, who died in 1778.

After Washington left the army in 1783 and returned to Mount Vernon, he and Martha entertained constantly. French general Lafayette (at left) was one of their guests.

The Road to Union

☆ ☆

After the Revolution, the hard work began. Now that Americans had won their independence from Britain, it would be necessary to form a new government to replace British rule. It was an overwhelming task that did not go smoothly. There were still no united states because no one could agree on the terms that would unite them. Each state, in fact, considered itself an independent nation. They even issued their own money! Imagine the confusion when leaders called a convention in Philadelphia in 1787 to tackle the issues. Should there be a strong central government? Should the states be independent? Should America, like Europe, be a patchwork of countries or come together under one leader? Finally, after a hot summer of debate and compromise, delegates crafted the Constitution, which contains laws for governing the country and describes how the government should be set up. It still guides us today and is the oldest national constitution in effect in the world.

It took nearly a year for enough states to approve the Constitution and agree to become the United States. However, many were concerned over the dangers of a powerful central government. They feared that the rights of individuals had not been guaranteed in this important document. At the suggestions of several states, James Madison drew up a list of ten basic rights to which all Americans would be entitled. They included freedom of religion, of speech, and of the press. These first ten amendments, or additions, to the Constitution are known as the Bill of Rights. They became part of the Constitution in 1791.

had successfully fought for and won their independence from Britain. Now the question was how the new, independent country should be governed. Sitting around the dinner table in Mount Vernon's fine new two-story banquet hall, George and his guests discussed this question endlessly.

Martha stayed out of these discussions as much as possible. In a letter to Fanny Bassett—who had married George's nephew and was now Fanny

George Washington, after having been unanimously elected the first president of the United States, arrived in New York to a hero's welcome.

Bassett Washington—dated February 25, 1788, Martha wrote, "We have not a single article of news but pollitick, which I do not conscern myself about . . ."

By early 1789, even Martha could no longer ignore "pollitick." Much as she and George might prefer to spend their lives in quiet retirement, it was becoming increasingly clear that the country still needed George's services. The hero of the Revolution was now named as the one man who could lead the new nation in peacetime.

Official notification arrived on April 14, 1789—George Washington had been unanimously elected first president of the United States of America. Within two days, a reluctant Washington set off for a job he had not

George Washington took the oath of office as the first president of the United States on April 30, 1789.

sought and was not at all sure he could master. Once again, Martha was left behind to attend to the details of moving. It was not a happy duty. As she wrote to her nephew John Dandridge, "My Dear John, I am truly sorry to tell that the General is gone to New York . . . when, or wheather he will ever come home again God only knows—I think it was much too late for him to go in to publick life again, but it was not to be avoided; our family will be deranged as I must soon follow him . . . I am greved at parting . . ."

CHAPTER SIX

The Presidency

* * * * * * * * * * * * * * * * *

Martha Washington may have been grieved at leaving Mount Vernon, but she didn't allow personal unhappiness to interfere with public responsibility. George would never think of shirking his duty to his country, and Martha would never think of shirking her duty to George. Briskly and competently, she made arrangements to move to the country's temporary capital in New York City.

The children, ten-year-old Nelly and eight-year-old Wash, would come with her. Fanny and her husband, George Augustine, agreed to stay on to manage things at Mount Vernon. It took a full month of packing,

* * * * * * * * * * * * * * * * *

This three-story rented house at 3 Cherry Street in New York City was the home of President George Washington and his wife Martha.

sorting, and planning, but by May 16, 1789, Martha, Nelly, and Wash were on their way.

It was quite a journey. The children were excited by the crowds of enthusiastic citizens they met all along the way—and by the runaway horses, dangerous river crossings, and treacherous currents that nearly overturned their ferry across the Potomac River.

Martha took the excitement in stride. As she wrote to Fanny, "I have the pleasure to tell you, that we had a very agreable journey . . ." She, too, was touched by the outpouring of affection that greeted her at every stage of the journey. She was entertained with balls and dinners, bands and parades, cheering crowds and a thirteen-gun salute. By the time she reached New York City, there could be no doubt that "Lady Washington," as she was enthusiastically hailed, was a great favorite with the American citizenry.

As First Lady, Martha Washington helped her husband, the president, arrange afternoon receptions, evening receptions, and official dinners.

Martha was overwhelmed with responsibilities in New York. She quickly organized the three-story rented house at 3 Cherry Street, where the family would live and where George would have his offices. She helped George arrange regular Tuesday afternoon receptions, or "levees," to which only men were invited. She began holding her own Friday evening receptions, called "drawing rooms," which were open to men and women, and which the president also attended. She received morning callers and paid her own formal visits in return. She hosted weekly Thursday night official dinners (where she frequently served that favorite new dessert called ice cream) and gave additional dinner parties for government officials and foreign visitors.

"I have not had one half hour to myself since the day of my arrival," she wrote to Fanny. But as the next line of

Their Majesties

✫ ✫

Amid the hubbub of inventing a new nation, one particularly gnarly problem loomed. What should the president and his wife be called? How should they be addressed? Since America was attempting to forge a democracy free from any hint of monarchy, most royal titles seemed inappropriate. Congress hotly debated the issue. Vice President John Adams and others who believed that the office called for an impressive title suggested "His Highness" as the correct address for the president and "the Presidentress" for his wife. Others softened the royal tone by advocating "His Elective Highness" and "His Patriotic Majesty." To some, the debate seemed comic, and they proposed that the portly vice president himself be addressed as "His Rotundity." The discussion embarrassed the Washingtons, and in the end Congress decided on the straightforward "President of the United States" as the executive title. Martha became known as "Lady Washington." The term "First Lady" did not come into use for another sixty years. Perhaps the best measure of the Washingtons' status as ordinary Americans appeared in the Philadelphia city directory for 1796, which listed "WASHINGTON, GEORGE, President of the United States, 190 High Street" in alphabetical order between "Warts, John, sea-captain, near 19 Vernon Street" and "Wastlie, John, skindresser, 53 So. Fifth Street." Only capital letters distinguished the chief executive from the sailor and the leatherworker.

her letter reveals, family was always Martha's main preoccupation. "My first care was to get the children to a good school, which they are boath very much pleased at."

Martha Washington had no guide to follow as the wife of an American president. She was very much aware that her behavior would set a precedent for future First Ladies. She recognized her responsibility to be an example that would do the American people proud, in their own eyes and in the eyes of the rest of the world. In

Abigail Adams, wife of Vice President John Adams, was impressed with Martha Washington.

Washington in conference with the members of his first cabinet

Vice President John Adams

everything she did, Martha struggled to find a balance between the formality and decorum required by her position, and her own natural warmth and friendliness.

One person who was impressed was Abigail Adams, wife of Vice President John Adams. Abigail Adams sat next to Martha at the Friday evening receptions, and her shrewd eye missed little. "She is plain in her dress, but that plainness is the best of every article," Abigail wrote to her sister. "Her man-

This gown worn by First Lady Martha Washington is displayed in the Smithsonian Institution.

impressed Abigail with her maternal affections. In that same letter, Abigail wrote, "Mrs. Washington is . . . doatingly fond of her Grandchildren, to whom she is quite the Grandmamma."

Being always in the public eye was a strain for Martha. George had decided they should not accept private social invitations, and the constant schedule of public entertaining was wearing. By October of 1789, Martha was writing to Fanny, "I think I am more like a state prisoner than anything else. There are certain bonds set for me which I must not depart from . . ."

Generally, however, Martha maintained her characteristic good humor. There was no question that she—and George, for that matter—would rather be home at Mount Vernon. But there was also no question that they would each willingly obey "the voice of their country," as Martha put it. As she wrote to another friend, Mercy Otis Warren, "I do not . . . feel dissatisfied with my present station— no, God forbid—for everybody and everything conspire to make me as

ners are modest and unassuming, dignified and femenine . . . no lady can be more deservedly beloved and esteemed as she is."

As might be expected, Martha also

Mercy Otis Warren (1728–1814)

★ ★ ★ ★ ★ ★ ★ ★ ★ ★ ★ ★ ★ ★ ★ ★ ★ ★ ★ ★

As the daughter of a prominent family in Barnstable, Massachusetts, Otis received more than the usual female education in keeping house, sharing her brother James's tutor. As a young mother, her literary talents and patriotic sensibilities emerged in poetic form; her poem "The Squabble of the Sea Nymphs" about the Boston Tea Party came out to wide acclaim in the *Boston Gazette*. In plays and poetry, she poked fun at the royal governor of Massachusetts and others loyal to Great Britain. In one poem, she appealed to women not to buy British goods by giving up "feathers, furs, rich sattins and du capes/And head dresses in pyramidal shapes." In *The Motley Assembly*, Mercy made history by writing the first play in America about Americans. She wrote her political satire under an assumed name, since such compositions were deemed inappropriate for women. However, she did publish her greatest work, a three-volume history of

the Revolution, under her own name in 1805. The project took thirty years to complete and made Mercy one of the first historians to document the War of Independence.

contented as possable in it. . . . I am still determined to be cheerful and to be happy in whatever situation I may be, for I have also learnt from experianence that the greater part of our happiness or misary depends upon our dispositions, and not upon our circumstances; we carry the seeds of the one or the other about with us, in our minds, wherever we go."

As always, Martha was concerned about George's health and comfort. Being the first president of a new nation was both exciting and exhausting. George Washington had no model to follow as he tried to establish a strong, orderly government. He wrote to a friend early in his presidency that few "can realize the difficult and delicate part which a man in my situation has to act . . . my station is new; and, if I may use the expression, I walk on untrodden ground."

Martha made sure that George had some relaxing family time each week. On Sundays, they took the children to church and on long carriage rides. All four of them frequently attended the small theater on John Street off Broadway. They visited the waxworks,

A portrait of George Washington, the first president of the new United States

where the children could see a statue of their grandfather in his Revolutionary War uniform.

Twice during the first year of his presidency, George Washington became seriously ill, and Martha dedicated herself to nursing him back to health. The story is told that she even had straw spread on the street in front of the house to muffle the sounds of passing carriages.

A portrait of Martha Dandridge Custis Washington, the first First Lady of the United States

In the spring of 1790, the Washingtons moved to Macomb House on Lower Broadway.

In the spring of 1790, the Washingtons moved to a larger house on lower Broadway Street. It was here that they hosted the nation's first official Fourth of July party, setting the precedent for future Independence Day celebrations. Martha and George served wine and cake to hundreds of visitors, and the day ended with a brilliant display of fireworks over the Hudson River.

By August of 1790, Martha was packing up her household again. Congress had voted to move the nation's capital to a new Federal City being built along the banks of the Potomac River. Until this capital was ready, the seat of government would move to Philadelphia. Martha was looking forward to the move to Philadelphia, a city that she knew from Revolutionary War days. Even more, she was looking forward to the two-month vacation she and George would have at Mount Vernon before the move.

Mount Vernon was never far from either of the Washingtons' thoughts throughout the

From Mud and Flames

⭐ ⭐

Though President Washington would never live in the city that bears his name, he was very much involved in its creation. When Congress empowered him to choose a site for the nation's permanent capital in 1790, he selected one along the swampy banks of the Potomac River not far from Mount Vernon. President Washington then asked architect Pierre L'Enfant to draw up the plans. L'Enfant's grand scheme included boulevards, monumental buildings, and circular plazas. At its center stood the Capitol, or "Congress House." For the "President's Palace," President

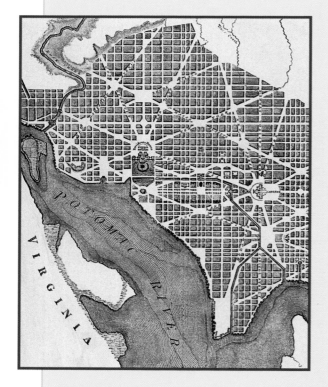

Washington requested "the sumptuousness of a palace, the convenience of a house, and the agreeableness of a county seat." By 1800, enough of the city stood to move the government from Philadelphia, in time for the presidency of John Adams. Congressmen found Washington a rugged town. Run-down houses, tree stumps, rubbish heaps, and muddy streets contrasted with the elegant public buildings. The city was still under construction when the British burned it during the War of 1812. The flames gutted both the President's House and the Capitol, and it took a long time to rebuild the capital city. Painted white to cover the burn marks, the President's House earned the name White House. In 1819, Congress moved back to an expanded Capitol. Construction there continued for years to produce the great domed structure we know today.

A view of Philadephia's Second Street north from Market Street as it looked about the time George and Martha Washington arrived at the temporary seat of government

presidency. Both wrote frequently to Fanny and George Augustine, instructing them in the proper management of the plantation.

Martha relied on Mount Vernon to supply foods and services for the presidential households in New York and Philadelphia. Fanny sent hams and bacons, dried fish and fruits, and seeds for planting. She answered Martha's requests to have Mount Vernon seamstresses provide the laces, ruffles, and other fine needlework the absent first family needed for their temporary homes.

Martha was happier in Philadelphia than she had been in New York. For one thing, she was growing more comfortable in her role as First Lady. Then, too, Martha had friends in Philadelphia from the war days. George gradually relaxed his rule against accepting private invitations, and the two of them enjoyed many so-

Secretary of State Thomas Jefferson

Secretary of the Treasury Alexander Hamilton

ciable hours at parties, concerts, and the theater. But Philadelphia could never be the home that Mount Vernon was, and Martha was dismayed when it became obvious that George would be elected to serve a second term as president.

Like Martha, George Washington was ready to retire from public life. But he could see that the young American republic was in danger of splitting into two opposing sides. There were serious differences of opinion between Secretary of State Thomas Jefferson and Secretary of the Treasury Alexander Hamilton. When both sides told Washington that he was the only man who could keep the struggling government together, he reluctantly agreed to accept a second term.

George Washington was sworn in for his second term as president in March 1793. It was not a happy time for Martha. Besides the depressing prospect of another four years in Philadelphia, there was sorrowful news from Mount Vernon. George Augustine Washington, George's nephew and Fanny's husband, had

George Washington's second inauguration as president took place in Congress Hall in Philadelphia on March 4, 1793.

died the previous month, leaving Fanny with three young children.

Although her heart was full of thoughts for her beloved Fanny, Martha continued to fulfill her social obligations to her country. And, of course, she continued to take vigilant care of Nelly and Wash. By now, Nelly was a lively teenager who described herself as "harum scarum, sans soucie!" Wash, too, was charming and lively but, like his father before him, was spoiled and undisciplined.

Martha also worried about George. His second term of office was proving much more difficult than the first. There were Indian attacks on the frontier, a growing national debate

President Washington (right) in consultation with Secretary of State Thomas Jefferson (left) and Secretary of the Treasury Alexander Hamilton

over the question of slavery, and disagreements about policies with Great Britain and France. Most troubling of all were the increasingly heated arguments between Alexander Hamilton's Federalists and Thomas Jefferson's Republicans. When Jefferson finally resigned as secretary of state, Washington—himself a Federalist—was deluged with criticism.

Martha was furious. George had given his life to serve his country, and this was the thanks he got! For as long as she lived, Martha Washington would never again have a kind word to say about Thomas Jefferson.

By 1797, Martha and George Washington were more than ready to turn over the reins of government to President-Elect John Adams. Martha

On February 22, 1797, 12,000 people attended the retirement ball held on the president's sixty-fifth birthday.

was touched and honored on February 22, 1797, when 12,000 grateful citizens attended the retirement ball held on George's sixty-fifth birthday. But she was overjoyed two weeks later, when John Adams was sworn in as the new president. Finally, she and George were free.

CHAPTER SEVEN

"Under Our Own Roof"

✫ ✫ ✫ ✫ ✫ ✫ ✫ ✫ ✫ ✫ ✫ ✫ ✫ ✫

As always, it was wonderful to be home again, especially knowing that this time they were home for good. "We once more . . . got seated under our own Roof, more like new beginners than old established residenters," Martha wrote to a friend. She added, "We found . . . all the buildings in a decaying state."

George quickly set about the business of restoring his neglected buildings and farmlands. He was as relieved as Martha to be through with public duty. As eighteen-year-old Nelly wrote to a friend, "Grandpapa is very well, and much pleased with being once more Farmer Washington."

✫ ✫ ✫ ✫ ✫ ✫ ✫ ✫ ✫ ✫ ✫ ✫ ✫ ✫

Farmer George Washington, joined by his grandchildren Nelly and Wash, supervising the workers on his Mount Vernon plantation

Of course Martha was happy to be at Mount Vernon. But even now, her joy at finally coming home was tinged with sorrow. For just a year earlier, Martha's beloved niece Fanny had died. Martha and George remained honorary grandparents to Fanny's children all their lives.

Martha soon found herself acting as hostess to an endless stream of houseguests. It seemed that everyone—friends, relatives, even strangers—wanted to visit the nation's first president under his own roof. Ruefully, Martha realized that she and George were celebrities, and that they would never really live a totally private life.

At least Martha still had Nelly and Wash to mother and coddle. Nelly was by now an attractive, vivacious young woman who loved tea parties, the theater, horse races, and balls. With Martha's blessing, Nelly frequently visited her two older sisters. Both Eliza and Patty were now married and had families of their own in nearby Georgetown.

Wash was another matter. Like his father before him, Wash preferred dogs and horses to books and studying. He attended Princeton University in New Jersey and then St. John's College in Annapolis, but it was clear he had neither the aptitude nor the discipline for advanced studies. When Wash finally came back to Mount Vernon to live in August 1798, George was disappointed that he had dropped out of school. Martha was simply happy to have him home.

George and Martha could both rejoice a few months later, when Nelly announced that she had fallen in love with George's nephew, Lawrence Lewis. Nelly wanted to be married on February 22, 1799—the sixty-seventh birthday of her step-grandfather. George was touched. He even donned his old Revolutionary War uniform to give the bride away in a simple candlelight ceremony at Mount Vernon.

Both Washingtons were pleased when the young couple chose to make their home at Mount Vernon. They were even more pleased when Nelly

George and Martha Washington thoroughly enjoyed having their family around them during their retirement years at Mount Vernon.

The Washingtons and Slavery

★ ★

Both George and Martha Washington grew up in a society that depended on slavery. Just before the Revolution, nearly 500,000 slaves toiled in colonial households and fields, mostly in the South. The Washingtons themselves ran Mount Vernon profitably on the free labor provided by nearly 300 slaves. George was a demanding master, taking a personal role in directing work in the fields with his overseer. When he pleaded with the Continental Congress to allow blacks to fight in the Revolutionary army, his primary reason was to keep them from fighting for the British. Indeed, many blacks did enlist with the British, who promised them freedom in exchange. Over the years, Washington's attitude toward slavery changed. As the young country struggled with issues of equality and freedom, many Americans, including Washington, began to question the role played by slavery. After the war, Washington, perhaps influenced by New York's strong antislavery movement, wrote to a friend that he would never again purchase another slave. As president, Washington's first priority was to keep the country together in its early years, and he favored a slow, orderly dismantling of the institution of slavery. In his will, Washington asked that all his slaves be freed, and educated, on Martha's death. Martha herself freed many of the slaves in 1800, though Virginia law forbade their schooling. George Washington's will can be taken as a sign of his final attitude toward slavery and the people who had served him in his plantation fields, in the fields of war, and throughout his life.

gave birth to a healthy daughter on November 27, 1799. Babies were always the best part of life for Martha, and little Frances Parke Lewis quickly became a favorite with her great-grandmama.

Once again, however, sorrow soon followed joy for Martha Washington. On December 12, 1799, George Washington rode horseback around his farmlands for five hours. As he noted in his diary that day, "About 10

George Washington, in his Revolutionary War uniform, gave the bride away when his granddaughter Nelly married Lawrence Lewis.

o'clock it began to snow, soon after to Hail, and then to a settled cold Rain."

The next day, George's throat was sore, and by nighttime his breathing had become labored. Alarmed, Martha immediately sent for the doctor. Unfortunately, there was nothing to be done. For twenty-four hours, Martha stayed close by her husband's side. Then, about 10:30 on the night of December 14, George Washington died.

Martha felt dazed and crushed. "I only wish soon to follow him," she is

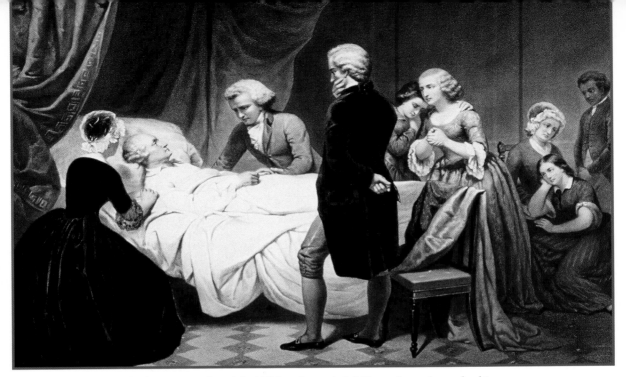

George Washington died on December 14, 1799, after a brief illness brought on by his exposure to snow, hail, and a cold rain while riding around his farmlands two days earlier.

reported to have said. "My last painful task is over."

Letters of condolence poured into Mount Vernon as an entire nation mourned the death of its first president. Among them was a letter from President John Adams, asking a painful favor of the grieving widow. Upon hearing of Washington's death, Congress had passed a resolution to build a marble sarcophagus in the new Capitol in Washington, D.C. Now President Adams wanted Martha's permission to bury George Washing-

ton—the nation's first president—under that marble monument.

Martha knew George had wanted to be buried at his beloved Mount Vernon. And certainly she wanted nothing more than to have her life's partner laid to rest in the family vault. But George had spent his entire life obeying the voice of his country, and now Martha felt compelled to do the same.

On December 31, 1799—the last day of the eighteenth century—Martha Washington sadly and bravely wrote back to President Adams: "Taught by the great example which I have so long had before me never to oppose my private wishes to the public will, I must consent to the request made by Congress, which you have had the goodness to transmit to me, and in doing this I need not—I cannot say what a sacrifice of individual feeling I make to a sense of public duty."

As it turned out, Martha was never called upon to make this final sacrifice. Today, George Washington's tomb remains at his home in Mount Vernon.

After George's death, Martha lost much of her spirit and interest in life. She continued her role as a gracious hostess to the hundreds of visitors who now came to Mount Vernon expressly to see her. Many of these visitors were Revolutionary War veterans who had never forgotten the kindness of "Lady Washington."

Martha was grateful to Nelly, Lawrence, and Wash, who all lived at Mount Vernon with her. She looked forward to visits and letters from other close friends and family. And she adored her great-granddaughters,

This miniature portrait of Martha Washington was made in 1801, about a year before she died.

Frances Parke and little Martha Betty, who was born in August 1781.

By the spring of 1802, Martha's health was failing. Conscientious to the last, she wrote out her will—and then burned almost all of the letters she and George had written to each other. Some things, at least, would remain private.

On May 22, 1802, with a loving Nelly by her side, Martha died of "severe fever." She was seventy years old.

For forty years, Martha Washington was a constant, supportive com-

Profile of America, 1802: Young America

✯ ✯

By the time Martha Washington died in 1802, Thomas Jefferson, the third president of the United States, held office. The national seat of government had by then been moved to the brand-new capital—Washington, D.C. Though the White House and the Capitol were unfinished and mud clogged the streets, the city slowly took shape. And so did the country.

America had been independent for just less than twenty years. While much had been accomplished in those first years, the difficulties of building a new nation from scratch were far from over. Americans struggled to apply the principles they had fought for in the Revolution, including liberty and self-governance. By 1802, the Constitution and Bill of Rights, written to outline the foundation of the new government, had been agreed on by all the states. But two political parties had emerged throughout the heated debate: the Federalists, who believed in a strong federal government, and the Republicans, who believed more in state and individual rights. Americans around 1802 were perhaps the first to endure the sense and nonsense of party politics.

Like their country, most of America's 5 million people were young, too. Their energy and self-confidence helped to form the American character; they had high hopes and ambitions for themselves and the nation. They were eager to explore the wilderness that lay beyond the cities and farmlands of the East Coast. The frontier—the edge of settlement—poked into the Ohio Valley, where fertile lands lured settlers west. People began to pour over the Appalachian Mountains in wagons and riverboats to probe the hills and hollows of Kentucky and Tennessee, the newest of the sixteen states. Cities like Pittsburgh, Pennsylvania, Cincinnati, Ohio, and Lexington, Kentucky, sprouted in the wilderness.

While white Americans left eagerly to find new homes in the West, Native Americans reluctantly retreated there because little room remained for them in the East. Though President Jefferson envisioned a large reservation for all the native peoples beyond the Mississippi River, the disorganized and displaced groups lingered on the fringes of white settlement and grew dependent on trade. Alcohol and disease decimated their numbers. While young America found her cultural identity, the Native Americans lost theirs. The issue of slavery, too, began to divide the nation. By 1802, most of the northern states had outlawed slavery. In the South, slave uprisings became more common as African-Americans in bondage sought to enjoy the freedom and equality promised to others in the new nation.

As early as 1802, issues and ideas that would both divide and unite Americans over the years were taking shape. Debates over equality, race, politics, the power of government, and the rights of the individual begun in America's youth rage on today.

panion to the man she loved. She was an exemplary wife and mother at a time when being a wife and mother was the highest goal a woman could reach.

Beyond this, Martha was a selfless and courageous patriot in her own right. She set a standard of gracious hospitality for future First Ladies and was a shining example of what it means to be a public servant. Perhaps the obituary that appeared in an Alexandria newspaper said it best: "She was the worthy partner of the worthiest of men."

Today, Martha and George Washington are entombed together in the family vault in Mount Vernon.

Martha and George Washington are buried together in the family vault at Mount Vernon.

95

The Presidents and Their First Ladies

YEARS IN OFFICE			
President	Birth–Death	First Lady	Birth–Death
1789–1797 George Washington	1732–1799	Martha Dandridge Custis Washington	1731–1802
1797–1801 John Adams	1735–1826	Abigail Smith Adams	1744–1818
1801–1809 Thomas Jefferson†	1743–1826		
1809–1817 James Madison	1751–1836	Dolley Payne Todd Madison	1768–1849
1817–1825 James Monroe	1758–1831	Elizabeth Kortright Monroe	1768–1830
1825–1829 John Quincy Adams	1767–1848	Louisa Catherine Johnson Adams	1775–1852
1829–1837 Andrew Jackson†	1767–1845		
1837–1841 Martin Van Buren†	1782–1862		
1841 William Henry Harrison‡	1773–1841		
1841–1845 John Tyler	1790–1862	Letitia Christian Tyler (1841–1842) Julia Gardiner Tyler (1844–1845)	1790–1842 1820–1889
1845–1849 James K. Polk	1795–1849	Sarah Childress Polk	1803–1891
1849–1850 Zachary Taylor	1784–1850	Margaret Mackall Smith Taylor	1788–1852
1850–1853 Millard Fillmore	1800–1874	Abigail Powers Fillmore	1798–1853
1853–1857 Franklin Pierce	1804–1869	Jane Means Appleton Pierce	1806–1863
1857–1861 James Buchanan*	1791–1868		
1861–1865 Abraham Lincoln	1809–1865	Mary Todd Lincoln	1818–1882
1865–1869 Andrew Johnson	1808–1875	Eliza McCardle Johnson	1810–1876
1869–1877 Ulysses S. Grant	1822–1885	Julia Dent Grant	1826–1902
1877–1881 Rutherford B. Hayes	1822–1893	Lucy Ware Webb Hayes	1831–1889
1881 James A. Garfield	1831–1881	Lucretia Rudolph Garfield	1832–1918
1881–1885 Chester A. Arthur†	1829–1886		

† wife died before he took office   ‡ wife too ill to accompany him to Washington   * never married

1885–1889			
Grover Cleveland	1837–1908	Frances Folsom Cleveland	1864–1947
1889–1893			
Benjamin Harrison	1833–1901	Caroline Lavinia Scott Harrison	1832–1892
1893–1897			
Grover Cleveland	1837–1908	Frances Folsom Cleveland	1864–1947
1897–1901			
William McKinley	1843–1901	Ida Saxton McKinley	1847–1907
1901–1909			
Theodore Roosevelt	1858–1919	Edith Kermit Carow Roosevelt	1861–1948
1909–1913			
William Howard Taft	1857–1930	Helen Herron Taft	1861–1943
1913–1921			
Woodrow Wilson	1856–1924	Ellen Louise Axson Wilson (1913–1914)	1860–1914
		Edith Bolling Galt Wilson (1915–1921)	1872–1961
1921–1923			
Warren G. Harding	1865–1923	Florence Kling Harding	1860–1924
1923–1929			
Calvin Coolidge	1872–1933	Grace Anna Goodhue Coolidge	1879–1957
1929–1933			
Herbert Hoover	1874–1964	Lou Henry Hoover	1874–1944
1933–1945			
Franklin D. Roosevelt	1882–1945	Anna Eleanor Roosevelt	1884–1962
1945–1953			
Harry S. Truman	1884–1972	Bess Wallace Truman	1885–1982
1953–1961			
Dwight D. Eisenhower	1890–1969	Mamie Geneva Doud Eisenhower	1896–1979
1961–1963			
John F. Kennedy	1917–1963	Jacqueline Bouvier Kennedy	1929–1994
1963–1969			
Lyndon B. Johnson	1908–1973	Claudia Taylor (Lady Bird) Johnson	1912–
1969–1974			
Richard Nixon	1913–1994	Patricia Ryan Nixon	1912–1993
1974–1977			
Gerald Ford	1913–	Elizabeth Bloomer Ford	1918–
1977–1981			
James Carter	1924–	Rosalynn Smith Carter	1927–
1981–1989			
Ronald Reagan	1911–	Nancy Davis Reagan	1923–
1989–1993			
George Bush	1924–	Barbara Pierce Bush	1925–
1993–			
William Jefferson Clinton	1946–	Hillary Rodham Clinton	1947–

Martha Dandridge Custis Washington Timeline

1731	✶	Martha Dandridge is born on June 21
1732	✶	George Washington is born on February 22
		Benjamin Franklin issues the first *Poor Richard's Almanac*
		James Oglethorpe founds Georgia, the thirteenth colony
1735	✶	John Zenger is acquitted in New York City
1738	✶	British troops settle border dispute with Spanish Florida
		Religious revival begins in colonial America
1739	✶	Three slave uprisings take place in South Carolina
1741	✶	First American symphony orchestra is organized in Bethlehem, Pennsylvania
		Great Awakening begins
1742	✶	Faneuil Hall opens in Boston
1744	✶	Iroquois cede Ohio River Valley to the British
		King George's War begins
1745	✶	Army of colonial New Englanders take Fort Louisbourg
1747	✶	New York Bar Association is founded
1748	✶	King George's War ends
1749	✶	Martha Dandridge marries Daniel Parke Custis
1750	✶	Estimated colonial population is 1,207,000
		Great Awakening ends
1751	✶	Daniel Custis is born
1752	✶	Benjamin Franklin conducts his electricity experiment
1753	✶	Daniel Custis dies
		Frances Custis is born

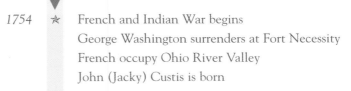

1754 ✷ French and Indian War begins
George Washington surrenders at Fort Necessity
French occupy Ohio River Valley
John (Jacky) Custis is born

1755 ✷ "Yankee Doodle" becomes a popular song

1756 ✷ Martha (Patsy) Custis is born

1757 ✷ Frances Custis dies
Daniel Parke Custis dies

1759 ✷ Martha Dandridge Custis marries George Washington and moves to Mount Vernon
French abandon Fort Ticonderoga
British defeat French at Quebec

1760 ✷ French surrender Montreal
British capture Detroit
Benjamin Franklin invents bifocal glasses

1763 ✷ Treaty of Paris ends French and Indian War
Britain gains Canada and French lands east of the Mississippi River

1765 ✷ British Parliament passes the Stamp Act
Colonists hold Stamp Act Congress

1766 ✷ Parliament repeals the Stamp Act

1767 ✷ Parliament passes the Townshend Act

1770 ✷ Boston Massacre takes place
Parliament repeals the Townshend Act
First American mental hospital opens in Williamsburg, Virginia

1771 ✷ *Encyclopedia Britannica* is first published

1772 ✷ Boston Assembly demands rights of colonies and threatens secession
Samuel Adams forms Committees of Correspondence

1773 ✷ Colonists in Boston dump tea into Boston Harbor
Martha (Patsy) Custis dies

1774	★	Parliament passes the Intolerable Acts
		Parliament closes Boston Harbor
		First Continental Congress meets in Philadelphia and votes to boycott British goods
1775	★	First shots of the Revolutionary War are fired at Lexington and Concord in Massachusetts
		Second Continental Congress meets in Philadelphia and names George Washington commander of the American army
		Patrick Henry proclaims "Give me liberty or give me death!" in a speech in the Virginia Assembly of Delegates
1776	★	Washington drives British troops out of Boston
		Members of Second Continental Congress sign the Declaration of Independence
		Washington defeats the Hessians at Battle of Trenton
1777	★	Washington defeats British at Princeton
1778	★	British leave Philadelphia
		Americans defeat British at Monmouth
1781	★	Articles of Confederation are ratified as a framework for governing the United States
		British surrender to George Washington at Yorktown
		John (Jacky) Custis dies
1783	★	Treaty of Paris ends the Revolutionary War
1786	★	First steamboat is built in America
1787	★	Northwest Ordinance is passed
		Constitutional Convention is held in Philadelphia
1788	★	U.S. Constitution is ratified by a majority of states
		New York City becomes the nation's capital
1789	★	Federalist party is formed
		First session of U.S. Congress opens
		George Washington is elected president
		George Washington is inaugurated as president
		Martha Washington moves to New York City

1790	☆	Washington, D.C., is founded
		Philadelphia becomes the nation's capital
		Martha Washington moves to Philadelphia
1791	☆	Bank of North America is founded
		Bill of Rights is added to the U.S. Constitution
		Vermont becomes a state
1792	☆	President Washington lays cornerstone for Capitol in Washington, D.C.
		Construction begins on the White House
		The Farmer's Almanac is published
		Washington is reelected president
		New York Stock Exchange opens
		Kentucky becomes a state
1793	☆	Eli Whitney invents the cotton gin
1794	☆	Whisky Rebellion takes place in western Pennsylvania
		Eleventh amendment added to Constitution
1795	☆	President Washington signs the Naturalization Act
1796	☆	Tennessee becomes a state
		President Washington gives his Farewell Address
		John Adams is elected president
1798	☆	President Adams signs the Alien and Sedition Acts
		XYZ Affair takes place
		Eli Whitney introduces interchangeable parts
1799	☆	George Washington dies
1800	☆	John Adams moves the U.S. government to Washington, D.C.
		Thomas Jefferson is elected president
		Library of Congress is founded
1801	☆	Robert Fulton invents the submarine
1802	☆	U.S. Military Academy opens at West Point
		Martha Dandridge Custis Washington dies on May 22

Fast Facts about
Martha Dandridge Custis Washington

Born: June 2, 1731, on Chestnut Grove Plantation near Williamsburg, Virginia

Died: May 22, 1802, at Mount Vernon, Virginia

Burial Site: Mount Vernon, Virginia

Parents: John Dandridge and Frances Jones Dandridge

Education: Had no formal education but was taught to read and write at home; learned sewing and other household skills from her mother

Marriages: To Daniel Parke Custis, from 1749 until his death in 1757; to George Washington, from January 6, 1759 until his death on December 14, 1799

Children: Daniel Custis (1751–1753), Frances Custis (1753–1757), John (Jacky) Custis (1754–1781), Martha (Patsy) Custis (1756–1773); raised grandchildren Eleanor (Nellie) Custis and George Washington (Wash) Parke Custis

Places She Lived: Williamsburg, Virginia (1731–1759); Mount Vernon (1759–1802); New York City (1789–1790); Philadelphia (1790–1797)

Major Achievements:

* Held a smallpox inoculation clinic at Mount Vernon during the summer of 1777.
* Encouraged her husband and his troops during the Revolutionary War by spending the winter months at their encampments.
* Arranged receptions on Tuesday afternoons so that President Washington could meet with important men.
* Hosted official dinners on Thursday nights and other dinner parties for government officials and foreign visitors.
* Held Friday evening receptions that were open to both men and women.
* In New York with her husband, hosted the nation's first official Fourth of July party (1790).

Fast Facts about
George Washington's Presidency

Terms of Office: Elected in 1789 and reelected in 1792; served as the first president of the United States from 1789 to 1797

Vice President: John Adams (1789–1797)

Major Policy Decisions and Legislation:

* Signed the first act of Congress (June 1, 1789), which said that members of Congress and all officials of the federal and state governments would take an oath of allegiance before taking office.
* Signed acts establishing the state, war, and treasury departments.
* Signed the Judiciary Act, which provided for a six-member Supreme Court and established the office of attorney general.
* Appointed the first chief justice of the Supreme Court, John Jay, and the first five associate justices.
* Signed the first Census Act.
* Signed the first Patent Act and the first Copyright Act.
* Signed the first Naturalization Act, which set up requirements for U.S. citizenship.
* Signed the Jay Treaty.

Major Events:

* North Carolina and Rhode Island ratified the U.S. Constitution.
* Bill of Rights added to the U.S. Constitution.
* Vermont, Kentucky, and Tennessee were admitted to the Union as the fourteenth, fifteenth, and sixteenth states.
* The cornerstone of the presidential mansion (now called the White House) was laid on October 13, 1792.
* President Washington laid the cornerstone for the Capitol in Washington, D.C., on September 18, 1793.
* Whisky Rebellion took place in western Pennsylvania (July–November 1794).
* General "Mad" Anthony Wayne defeated the Miami Indians at Fallen Timbers, Ohio (August 20, 1794).

Where to Visit

The Capitol
Constitution Avenue
Washington, D.C. 20510
(202) 225-3121

George Washington Birthplace
    National Monument
1732 Popes Creek Road
Washington's Birthplace, Virginia
    22443
(804) 224-1732

Mount Vernon
Mount Vernon, Virginia 22121
(703) 780-2000

Museum of American History of the
    Smithsonian Institution
    "First Ladies: Political and Public
    Image"
14th Street and Constitution Avenue
    NW
Washington, D.C.
(202) 357-2008

National Archives
Constitution Avenue
Washington, D.C.
(202) 501-5000

The National First Ladies Library
The Saxton McKinley House
331 S. Market Avenue
Canton, Ohio 44702

White House
1600 Pennsylvania Avenue
Washington, D.C. 20500
Visitor's Office: (202) 456-7041

White House Historical Association
740 Jackson Place NW
Washington, D.C. 20503
(202) 737-8292

Online Sites of Interest

The First Ladies of the United States of America
http://www2.whitehouse.gov/WH/glimpse/firstladies/html/firstladies.html
A portrait and biographical sketch of each First Lady plus links to other White House sites.

George Washington Birthplace National Monument
http://www.nps.gov/gewa/
At George Washington's Birthplace in Westmoreland County, Virginia, the National Park Service interprets the childhood setting that influenced Washington's formative years. The site has links to a tour of the historic area, Washington family history, exhibits of Washington family artifacts, the family burial site, and more.

Internet Public Library, Presidents of the United States (IPL POTUS)
http://www.ipl.org/ref/POTUS/gwashington.html
An excellent site with much information on George Washington, including personal information and facts about his presidency; many links to other sites including biographies and other Internet resources.

Mount Vernon
http://www.mountvernon.org/
Includes a visitors' guide, a tour, educational resources, a description of the library and collections; and information on the archaeology program, which has explored several Mount Vernon sites.

The National First Ladies Library
http://www.firstladies.org
A virtual library devoted to America's First Ladies; includes a bibliography of material on the nation's First Ladies and a tour of the Saxton McKinley House in Canton, Ohio, which houses the library.

The White House
http://www.whitehouse.gov/WH/Welcome.html
Information about the current president and vice president; White House history and tours; biographies of past presidents and their families; a tour; and more.

The White House for Kids
http://www.whitehouse.gov/WH/kids/html/kidshome.html
Includes information about White House kids; famous "First Pets;" historic moments of the presidency; several issues of a newsletter, and more.

For Further Reading

Alter, Judy and Mary Collins. *Mount Vernon*. Cornerstones of Freedom. Danbury, Conn.: Children's Press, 1998.

Anderson, La Vere. *Martha Washington: First Lady of the Land*. A Discovery Biography. New York: Chelsea Juniors, 1991.

Fradin, Dennis Brindell. *Virginia*. From Sea to Shining Sea series. Chicago: Childrens Press, 1992.

Gormley, Beatrice. *First Ladies*. New York: Scholastic, Inc., 1997.

Gould, Lewis L. (ed.). *American First Ladies: Their Lives and Their Legacy*. New York: Garland Publishing, 1996.

Kent, Zachary. *George Washington: First President of the United States*. Encyclopedia of Presidents. Chicago: Childrens Press, 1986.

Klapthor, Margaret Brown. *The First Ladies*. 8th edition. Washington, D.C.: White House Historical Association, 1995.

Lukes, Bonnie L. *The American Revolution*. World History Series. San Diego: Lucent Books, Inc., 1996.

Mayo, Edith P. (ed.). *The Smithsonian Book of the First Ladies: Their Lives, Times, and Issues*. New York: Henry Holt, 1996.

McPherson, Stephanie Sammartino. *Martha Washington: First Lady*. Historical American Biographies. Springfield, N.J.: Enslow Publishers, Inc., 1998.

Meltzer, Milton. *George Washington and the Birth of Our Nation*. New York: Franklin Watts, 1986.

Paletta, Lu Ann. *World Almanac of First Ladies*. New York: World Almanac, 1990.

Sandak, Cass R. *The Washingtons*. New York: Crestwood House, 1991.

Siegel, Beatrice. *George and Martha Washington at Home in New York*. New York: Four Winds Press, 1989.

Index

Page numbers in **boldface type** indicate illustrations

Photo Identifications

Cover: Detail of the Eliphalet F. Andrews portrait of Martha Washington that hangs in the East Room of the White House

Page 8:   Portraits of George and Martha Washington, 1776, by C. W. Peale

Page 14:   Martha Washington in her younger days

Page 22:   Martha Washington

Page 42:   George Washington, 1775

Page 60:   George and Martha Washington with their grandchildren Nellie and Wash

Page 70:   Full-length portraits of First Lady Martha Washington by E. F. Andrews and President George Washington by Gilbert Stuart

Page 86:   A portrait of Martha Washington by James Peale

Photo Credits©

About the Author

Charnan Simon began her publishing career in Boston, in the children's book division of Little, Brown and Company. She then spent six rewarding years as an editor of *Cricket* Magazine, where she read thousands of stories and poems for children and worked with some of the most talented authors and artists in the world.

All of this was a tremendous help to Ms. Simon when she began writing her own books for young readers. Ms. Simon's academic background was also very useful. By earning both a Bachelor's and a Master's degree in English literature, Ms. Simon learned how to do original research and really use libraries. Today, she loves spending hours in libraries and historical societies, reading everything she can on the subject about which she is writing.

In doing the research for this book, Ms. Simon thoroughly enjoyed visiting Martha Washington's beloved Mount Vernon. She also loved reading the many letters Martha Washington wrote to her friends and relatives. Ms. Simon feels very fortunate to be able to share what she has learned about this girl from Virginia who became the nation's very first First Lady.

Charnan Simon lives in Madison, Wisconsin, with her husband and two daughters. She has written dozens of books for young people and particularly likes writing biographies of notable men and women who have helped shape our country and our world. When she is not busy writing books, Ms. Simon enjoys reading, gardening, and spending time with her family.